CW01653298

The *essential* Pocket KIWI

The *essential* Pocket KIWI

Nicholas Tarling

with cartoons by Guy Body

The Dunmore Press Ltd

First published in 1995
by
The Dunmore Press Ltd
P.O. Box 5115
Palmerston North
New Zealand

Australian Supplier:
Federation Press
P.O. Box 45
Annandale 2038 NSW
Australia
Ph: (02) 552-2200

ISBN 0 86469 258 7

Text:	Footlight MT 10.5/13
Printer:	The Dunmore Printing Company Ltd, Palmerston North
Cartoons:	Guy Body
Cover:	Stephanie Milne

Contents

Introduction

Kiwis have told themselves and told others what Kiwis were like. Are they still the same?

Change, if not decay, is all around. Has that changed the way Kiwis see themselves and the way others see them?

Written for Kiwis, but even more for those who are curious about Kiwis, this little book is a bit bigger than a squib and much less than an encyclopaedia.

It is written in the recognition that the debate cannot always be light-hearted but need not always be heavy-handed.

Of Kiwis and the Rest of the World

Let's give it a go. The Kiwi is ready to try his or her hand at anything. If a thing is worth doing, it is worth doing well, the old saying runs. The Kiwi version is different. Whether a thing is worth doing or not, it is worth having a go.

That applies whether or not others have tried it. If they have, it is surely possible and indeed necessary, to be the equal of the best in the world. And if they have not tried it, trying it will be yet another way in which New Zealand leads the world.

The Kiwi is practical. The big inventions may come from elsewhere. The Kiwi is good at applying them. And at mis-applying them, too. Where else would you

find a neighbour who had the stereo on in the back garden while using a mechanical saw? Is it possible to use a cellphone, eat a banana and drive a car all at the same time?

Almost anything can be fixed by a piece of 4 × 2 and a length of No. 8 fencing wire. That is a belief Kiwis have derived from their pioneering past. Perhaps it was never more than a myth. It has become less true, as machines have become more complex and more costly. But fixing it up, getting it going again, keeping it on the road, are still talents widely admired.

Just as well. The Kiwi feels ashamed to call a plumber in to fix a washer or an electrician to fix a fuse. In turn they are likely to be too disgusted to come. But if they eventually do, their bill reflects no sense of shame.

The Kiwi is a caring creature: she and even he are concerned people. Although their hospitals have become Crown Health Enterprises, Kiwis believe health care should be available for all. Although they have almost eliminated their natural forests, they, especially the 'greenies', are concerned about the environment and particularly about what other people are doing to theirs.

The Kiwi, though flightless, loves to fly. It wants to migrate, but often, like a godwit, to return, if only to leave again. Overseas experience (O.E.) is a rite of passage. Travel broadens the mind. It is certainly easier than learning a foreign language, although the young often travel the hard way and by the hardest route.

New Zealanders are good international citizens. They are pillars of great international organisations, such as U.N.E.S.C.O. and Oxford University Press. They are stabbed in Johannesburg and captured in Kurdistan. They read the news on the BBC and they sing at Bayreuth. Their caterers are captured in Somalia and their soldiers serve in Bosnia. There are only 3.5 million of them in New Zealand, but how many are there elsewhere? 130,000 of working age in Australia alone, apart from children and those who have retired there. They took full advantage of the British Empire and New Zealand exports expats.

Australasia – Austral-asia – means southern Asia, but no Kiwi likes the term: it sounds too much like

Attitudes to Asia

Australia. Nor do Kiwis – apart from the Prime Minister when speaking in Tokyo – think of themselves as 'Asian', though they do tend to lump Asians together like the yellow hordes of the past, even those who want to 'understand Asia' or be 'Asia-literate'.

Kiwi writers have searched for their identity. If you have to do that, it suggests a crisis, but probably only for Kiwi writers. The great New Zealand novel is like the Loch Ness monster, oft talked-of, never seen, except by those who like to provoke.

The Kiwis fought in all the twentieth-century wars. Their losses, particularly in World War I, were disproportionately great. They love peace. Having no frontiers, they find it difficult to understand why the nations so furiously rage together. Surely discussion can resolve problems? They can be sentimental about the rest of the world.

The Kiwis put themselves through a punishing series of changes in the 1980s, associated with 'Rogernomics' (after Roger Douglas, the Minister of Finance) and the process, though slowed down, still continues. What they wrote of themselves and what others wrote of them, even as recently as the 1960s, may no longer be true. Perhaps, as a result, they are more uncertain of themselves than they were. Is it still Godzone (God's Own Country)? Or is it chasing after false gods?

They were always rather uncertain and so prone both to imitate others and consider themselves superior, both to fawn and condemn.

Distance lends enchantment to the view. To cross the Tasman is but 1,500 miles, no distance at all to an

Australian. New Zealand is far too near to notice. A useful dumping ground for surplus manufactures, a tourist attraction for those who cannot afford to go further (or even as far in Australia), a country still in the 1950s (the Australians being in the 1960s); also, incidentally, close partners (ANZACs) in two world wars and now joined in closer economic relations (CER).

For the British, New Zealand is as far as you can go without (even sooner than you might wish) being on the return journey. And it is enchanting. English is spoken, more or less. They can see the episodes of Coronation Street they missed. Fish and chips are available. It is different, but not foreign. And the sun often shines.

And if it is too far actually to see, the mind's eye of the English can capture a New Zealand that is loyal, monarchist, living by the values that they themselves admire all the more for having themselves abandoned. The Kiwis were more English than the English themselves, home and colonial, if one may talk shop: 'the brighter Britain of the South' that Mary Sinclair extolled. Are they still? The Prime Minister has raised the question of a Republic, but few have backed him.

Across the Pacific there lies not only a dateline but, also, it seems, a faultline. How else can one explain the failure of the Americans to distinguish Australia and New Zealand? Americans indeed believe that all countries should be the same, namely like the United States, and that they differ only in the extent to which they fail to measure up. But that can hardly excuse their inability to perceive the differences which

Australians and New Zealanders are at pains to emphasise. Can they really not see that in quaint old Australia the two-dollar coin is smaller than the one-dollar coin while in conventional old New Zealand it is larger?

For the Europeans, New Zealand is green. No matter that the green is produced by aerial top-dressing; and there is a worry about the ozone layer and skin cancer is common. It is certainly unlike the Ruhr, particularly now it has taken pains to destroy its industrial base.

Do Asians see New Zealand as part of Asia? Asians, as Kiwis often fail to recognise, have differing views: the countries and peoples it contains are after all different. But, if the New Zealander is trying to understand them better, there is no evidence that the contrary is true. New Zealand will provide the young Japanese with a cheap honeymoon and the middle-aged Japanese with a cheap golf course. And it will provide the businessman from Singapore, Taipeh and Hong Kong with some cheap urban property and many Chinese and Japanese with a chance to learn English. Visitors from Asian countries, however, will see the inside of Chinese and Japanese restaurants and of international hotels designed in Singapore and managed with international anonymity. They will be on guided tours of mud and alps. The Kiwi overseas will have tried harder.

Visitors will nevertheless be welcome, if at times exploited. 'This is the friendliest country in the world', Austin Mitchell wrote, 'a characteristic it is not advisable to question if you value your teeth.' Violence now is

Sophisticates

less of a joking matter, but New Zealand is nearer the Singapore end of the scale than the New York end.

The tourist icons are Mount Cook and sheep. Most Kiwis, however, live in big cities and hardly see sheep, let alone touch them, from one year to another. They are generally urban, though rarely urbane. But New Zealand's shearers do beat the Aussies.

Characterising a person is difficult enough. Characterising a nation is more difficult still. Characterising the Kiwis, they might themselves say, is 'not a problem'. Not a problem, as the Chinese proverb puts it: just impossible.

Egalitarianism they derive from their colonial past. You might well be glad to leave a class-conscious Britain. You might hope to find better opportunities. You might not want to see the old rigidities recreated.

Some, however, did. They had not left to avoid but to emulate. The gentry of the South Island, whom Stevan Eldred-Grigg has depicted, did just that. 'They were a little like the Russian aristocracy – they had grown rich from land and spent their wealth in an attempt to recreate a foreign culture .... They turned their land into power and status. Like Russian nobles, the southern gentry were stupefied by it.'

Some of their houses remain, like Larnach Castle in Dunedin, or Elloughton Grange, now a home for the elderly. But they were cut down by economic change and by political intervention, though Canterbury, known to Britain for its labelling of imported lamb, even so retained at least in its own eyes an air of gentlemanliness.

Cutting down tall trees was a major colonial endeavour: the colonists decimated the forests in a way the environmentally-conscious green Kiwis would prefer to forget and not to see others imitate. The countryside still has something of the look of a recent clearing: not wild, like the Scots, but less manicured than the English.

Cutting down tall poppies remained a preoccupation. Success in New Zealand is unlikely to win praise. Achievers will be cut down well below size by what is sometimes termed the Kiwi clobbering-machine. That is something the 1980s did not change. It was merely revamped.

It is a small place. Everyone knows you have feet of clay. It is a land without heroes. 'The Poms', sniffed the late Sir Keith Sinclair, 'look a man in the tie'. The Kiwis don't need to wear one.

There are plenty of exceptions to prove the rule. There are rewards. Royal honours are still available in New Zealand and they are coveted. Political support will qualify. Not blotting your copybook is important, not stepping out of line, not being on a committee that fails to follow the Treasury line. A balance will be sought. Is there a woman on the list? A Maori? A South Islander? The system is not at odds with the tall poppy syndrome: it encourages compliance. And in so small a community, it can be very influential.

A royal honour characteristically elicits some false modesty. The knighthood somehow rewards others in the team. 'I still want to be called Jack', insists the egalitarian new knight, fearing to be thought 'up himself': Sir Jack And Dame Jill. Leading government Ministers, apointed to the Privy Council, are 'Right Honourable'. Other Ministers like to be called 'Honourable'.

Wealth offers another exception. Even if it does not of itself earn an honour, it earns some respect. The stockmarket crash of 1987 has not entirely tarnished it. New Zealand entrepreneurs were not quite so free with others' money as their counterparts in Australia. Or, perhaps characteristically, they kept quieter about it. And they are not so numerous.

That helps. The wealthy can be seen as an exception, those who got through. And some of them play up to it, expressing, if not modesty, at least surprise at their

achievement, not always realising that others are surprised, too. They are cards, if not jokers.

Sporting achievement is another exception. Every kind of sport has its Kiwi participants. Coming first in any of them is the subject of congratulation. Success as an All Black still leads to success in business and politics. Brain and brawn are not necessarily incompatible, but it helps if the team backs you up. The triumph in the America's Cup of 1995 – black magic indeed – revived the ticker-tape welcome. Carefully graded honours followed.

Success in mental endeavour is, however, clearly much more questionable. In New Zealand, as elsewhere, turning it into a competition can help: Montana book awards and Mobil Song quests can produce winners. And winning is something that can be understood by punters and sportsmen. Even brass band competitions – and New Zealanders blow hard – are reported like the English football results.

Achieving distinction without winning is dubious: tall poppies of this sort will be ploughed right back in. Or destroyed in a continuous eradication campaign, as if they were opium that might threaten the masses.

Claims to egalitarianism are, of course, likely to conceal real inequality. In 1979 Dale Williams wrote of a Kiwi Class System. 'We're up to our terry-towelling beach hats in one.' It was a question of keeping up with the Joneses and knowing which Jones to keep up with. Those who in the 1980s attacked the welfare state of the 1930s took full advantage of this weakness. It suited the middle class to see New Zealanders as equal. They benefited most and others could hardly be thought to exist. Overthrowing the system has, however, helped those at the top. Those at the bottom it has made more numerous.

Conformity is not unique to New Zealanders but it is a speciality. In New Zealand as elsewhere, men dress as if sumptuary legislation were in force. A lorry driver must wear a black singlet, a farmer gumboots. Bankers and lawyers must wear suits. A student will take care to cut the right splits in a pair of jeans and will often not wear shoes. Uniforms are worn at schools: it is one of the few issues in New Zealand education that is strenuously debated. Maybe the habit lingers. One habit indeed remains among those who otherwise grow up: wearing shorts, even in windy Wellington.

Women are less formal: no one goes out to buy some potatoes in long white gloves as they do in Queensland. Perhaps they are less conformist, too. But they are, of course, the readier prey for international fashions, handed down by women's magazines, bought on a visit to David Jones, or made up by an imaginative designer in one of the many, all too impermanent, boutiques.

Conforming to fashionable thinking is more worrying than conforming to fashionable dressing. And New Zealanders succumb too readily and with too little argument. New Zealand in the 1980s saw a period of widespread reform. The main thought was not whether what was done was the right thing or even whether it was being done in the right way. Rather: it's your (or my) turn next.

Nor did the Kiwis take full advantage of their internationalism. Often the fashions in thinking, like those in dressing, come from overseas. That should give you time, even in the era of rapid communication, to assess them before adopting them. Have the Americans done what their economists say should be done or are they merely advocating that others should do it? Was Mrs Thatcher really a Thatcherite? Even when the experience of others enjoins you not to follow them, the Kiwi will set thoughtlessly out on the same track, picking up ideas as if out of bottles thrown up on remote shores (or picked up in the duty free). What is suitable for the wealthiest country in the world is not necessarily suitable for New Zealand anyway. It's a kind of globotomy.

Perhaps it is part of being modern. If others think you are still in the nineteenth century, you need to persuade them, or at least yourselves, that you are virtually in the twenty-first century. Every shop must have a computerised billing system. Every sportsman must have the latest equipment. A cyclist cannot be without the full paraphernalia: 12 gears, a helmet, colourful shorts, shaved legs. Never use your hands (or your brains) if a machine can do it. No wonder the Japanese find New Zealand a useful market, even for their second-hand cars. In fact New Zealanders think they can afford everything the great industrial countries can offer their citizens. And they come surprisingly near success.

Though not reflective, New Zealanders can be thoughtful. In times of difficulty, they will come to your help. Nor is their friendliness, when shown, superficial. First names will come, if not first, then sooner than the British will expect. That can be convenient: first names are more easily remembered. But they are a sign of sincerity rather than, as you can feel in the U.S., of the reverse.

Most people have more common sense than their political leaders believe. The same is, fortunately, true of the Kiwis. They have a sense of humour, too, which helps them to put up with those leaders, though insufficiently often to challenge them.

'Of humour, except the unconscious variety, there is almost none', E.M. Smith wrote in 1939, and Dan Davin complained of its rarity. It is more private than public, almost samizdat at times. But New Zealand has produced some of the best cartoonists: Low who went away and Minhinnick who stayed at home and Bromhead who came and stayed.

And it has had and has its humorists: Glover and Fairburn, Gordon McLauchlan and Helen Brown, Denis Welch and A.K. Grant, Raybon Kan. Recommended reading.

Kiwis are not identified by class or accent. They are individuals, identified by what other individuals think about them. Their society is for the most part decent and orderly. But there is a vein of anarchy running through them.

Of Commercialism, Conformity and Common Sense

The Aussie pines for the bush but takes care not to live there. Inhabiting the most urban of countries, the Australians do not care to think their values are suburban. Something of the same paradox faces those who observe the Kiwi in its native habitat.

The New Zealand cities have their boutiques, their malls, their restaurants. You can hear the string quartet and the symphony orchestra. Tall office buildings are filled with recycled air. Even traffic jams can be managed (and mismanaged).

Is that the life for your real Kiwi jokers? Yes, in fact. But maybe they can get away from it all.

Be fair. You will find your Kiwis tramping in the bush (sometimes you will find them getting lost and

then it's national news and rescue services are set to work). You will find your Kiwis taking to the surf (and thoughtlessly enough, often the most dangerous surf, on a deceptively beautiful coastline where the sea can be a menace as well as a delight, the resort of merpersons). You will find your Kiwis on a boat or on the rocks (sometimes dangerously too) trying to tempt the fish that have escaped the drift-netting Asians (and smoked fish is delicious).

But are they really getting away from it all? The holiday 'bach' (or 'crib' in the South Island) becomes like a suburban home: the Kiwis take their motormowers on vacation. And your fishing vessel might well be really the firm's, run on an expense account, unless you can afford your own floating gin-palace.

What use is a fast train, Matthew Arnold asked, if it takes you from a dismal and illiberal life in Islington to a dismal and illiberal life in Camberwell? In New Zealand there are no fast trains (very few trains at all, in fact).

It was on Christmas Day 1814 that Samuel Marsden first preached the Christian gospel in New Zealand. Behold, he said, I bring you glad tidings of great joy. Maori and Pakeha sang the Old 100th Psalm.

The Maori said they could not understand what Marsden meant. But the missionaries were to enjoy considerable success. New Zealand was endowed with some wooden churches that are beautiful and rather fewer that are beautiful in stone and brick. Its religious life, within the Christian churches and outside, was lively and has remained so. Immigrants from Tonga and Samoa made the church the centre of their existence in a new land.

But the tidings of great joy that Marsden brought have also become tidings of excessive comfort. Christmas elsewhere has, of course, become highly commercialised. Gold, frankincense and myrrh may be hard to come by, but everything else is available at a price and everything else is deemed appropriate. 'It really is an atrocious institution, this Christmas', as Shaw snorted.

Commercialisation, however, could surely go no further than in New Zealand. The approach to this festival is marked by a deluge of advertising (and a characteristic feature of New Zealand commerce is its use of the junk mail approach). The media pour out carols (often, in the sweaty heat of Auckland, singing of reindeer and snow). And a card arrives from your insurance company (or the company that wants to be yours), with the assurance that after all the presents have been offered and the crackers popped and the guests gone, there will be always be – and the company gives its name, prudentially omitted from this book.

Christmas is a difficult time everywhere. It emphasises the loneliness of the lonely and it puts a strain on the relatives. 'I long for time to pass, so I can think of all this with nostalgia' (Peter de Vries). It tests our tolerance and challenges our benevolence and tries our patience. It is itself a temptation. In general, as Auden put it, we grossly overestimate our powers, to eat, to drink, to love our fellow persons.

In New Zealand Christmas is so much the worse for its coincidence with the height (or depth) of summer

and the prospect of a holiday. So panic-buying extends to food and drink as well as to gifts, to the necessary as well as the luxury (and the apparent fear of famine continues even though supermarkets are now open almost every day and much of the night).

The New Zealander wants to get away, to mow the lawn somewhere else, to try the surf, to bother the few remaining fish. Indeed, despite the supermarkets, the country tends to close down at the end of the year, opening a collective bleary eye sometime during January when the enticing prospect looms of getting the children back to school.

Googie Withers was said to have landed in New Zealand and found that it was closed. Things have changed. But somnolence certainly prevails after Christmas, as the country recovers from having hectically got ready to relax. It is broken only by boozy and sometimes raucous welcomes to the New Year. After all it arrives first in New Zealand (in Gisborne, more precisely).

No matter whether Marsden succeeded or not, the festival reflects the country's values. Commercialisation extends further. There is a frightening trend towards inventing a mid-winter Christmas as well as the mid-summer one. The 'market-driven' changes of the 1980s found a ready support. Almost any activity seeks sponsorship and almost anything can be turned to the advertiser's account. (This paragraph was sponsored by the Anti-Sponsorship Society.)

So we have the State *Insurance* Opera House and the New Zealand *Post* Youth Orchestra. In Auckland's

Aotea Centre, everything but the loo is sponsored (surely a missed opportunity for a splash): you enter a named auditorium after ascending a named staircase and going through a named lounge bar (at least some of the firms involved vanished after the 1987 crash and the naming is a marmoreal memorial).

Even the seventh-form school exam papers have carried an advertisement. Perhaps each question could be individually sponsored? (And maybe the successful scholar get a trip to Dunedin? Second prize, as the old joke has it: two trips to Dunedin.)

Has this market-driven frenzy destroyed the ability to relax that Kiwis prided themselves on? There was plenty of work in the 1950s and 1960s and living standards were high. Being able to relax was a sign of prosperity and achievement. It was something else that Kiwis could indeed do better than others.

Rest assured. It's still there. Perhaps, if it's possible to relax intensely, it's more intensely enjoyed than before. Maybe something hectic has got into this as well. But then there's something of Weimar about the rest of the world, too. Everything's for sale, everywhere. And the pursuit of leisure has become more frantic.

Professor Manfred Max-Neef believes Australia is the only country of which he can say: 'Every city is a beautiful city'. He meant, as he put it, that 'the people love their society, love their country and their city. There is a certain element of spirit and soul which is very difficult to find elsewhere'.

That may be a romantic view of the Aussie, though it has a core of truth. It could not be said of the Kiwi of

the 1990s, more uncertain, more quizzical. Not part of Asia; a bit disoriented.

Maybe a people is better off for lack of a grand plan, of an ideology, of a charismatic leader. But there is always a risk that something will fill a vacuum. We shall be manipulated by the media and cease to distinguish the real and the fictional. If most things can be bought or sold, so can our minds and souls.

You have, however, to reckon with Kiwi common sense and practicality. There's some irony around which is not always mere cynicism. And cutting them down to size has its positive side, too.

And if there are extremes to which the market might drive or the media might move, the Kiwi still wants to be sure that the other bloke (or the other sheila) is getting a fair go.

There are those, Bernard Levin reminded readers of the London *Times*, 'who would, if they had their way, make all of us live, think and act according to one sterile rule'; who fear and hate 'divergence, which is the most precious and the most significant of all our human qualities'.

Conformity in fashion, conformity in thinking: but the Kiwis do not rule out eccentricity. The real eccentric regards everyone else as an eccentric. Perhaps there are not many like this. Or maybe the Kiwis are all eccentrics.

For a start their land is a bit of an afterthought. Last, loneliest and loveliest, as, carried away by alliteration, the poet kindly put it. Indeed it is still being put together or blown apart by volcanic action. There is something eccentric about it. Earthquake precautions may help to keep the skyscrapers stable. What about the people?

The climate is eccentric, too. Its constant feature is the wind, worst in Wellington: it is like living on a ship, even though it's going nowhere. Little else is constant. Even if you can work out why winter is in June, July and August, you may find that the weather itself has second thoughts. Snow may after all fall in Dunedin on Boxing Day (but perhaps not on your first trip).

The flora are confused too. Indigenous forests have been largely destroyed. What remains of the original flora are appropriately cautious and slow-growing. But introduced flora are as ambivalent as new migrants. Some really take root, some do not. Some run riot and some dry up. Nor are they clear about the seasons. Some summer flowers will stick to Greenwich Mean Time. (What do Brussels sprouts do?) Others will go by the Kiwi calendar. Give it a grow.

Kiwis seem to share this eccentricity. You will find the men wearing shorts in the winter, looking as blue as children on the beach in an English summer. Shorts are, however, often associated with work. Work was largely manual and dressing for it looked as if you were clearly doing it and trying hard.

Some are, of course. Couriers really run: and so do refuse collectors, the fittest Kiwis of all. Running after the lorry, they throw the bags in as it moves along and then jump on themselves.

Maybe exertion is thought of mainly as physical rather than mental. A visitor observed that she never saw Kiwis walking: they were either driving or jogging.

The place is not crowded. Behaviour reflects that, too. Many or few, form a queue, said Billy Brown of London Town. Queueing is rare in New Zealand and, if it takes place, it is usually ignored.

Combined with conformity, there is eccentricity. Combined with order, there is more than a touch of anarchy. There are too many laws and, as a result, there is too much law-breaking; too many rules and regulations and too many infringements. The remedy tends to be sought in more rules and regulations. Not education.

New Zealand became known for some eccentrically gruesome murders. Now violence, as in other countries, seems to be increasing. The burglar uses his crowbar on the burgled. The police display their weapons and now and then use them too. Juvenile and post-juvenile gangs build what are little less than forts. Teenagers are drunk and mere kids sniff glue.

None of this is seen, of course, as a proper part of Kiwi life. Remedies, however, do not come to mind. Putting it right might come to be associated with a more draconian state. If violence is not far below the surface of order and decency, authoritarianism lurks under liberalism. Calls for law and order are popular. The confrontations over the Springbok tour in 1981 more than hinted at what that could mean.

The Kiwi lives an outdoor life in theory. In practice that may be limited to mowing the lawn and cleaning the car. Food, drink and TV are popular alternatives. Who actually plays rugby? Despite the prices they are charged for books, Kiwis buy a lot of them. Their own standards of publication are remarkably high.

Stoutly individual, the Kiwis, like everyone else, borrow from the Americans. If the Americans stop being a melting pot, then the Kiwis also seek a multicultural society. If they become more litigious, then barristers and solicitors flourish on the outer edge of the Pacific rim. A residual level-headedness, a touch of humour and a bit of pride may avert the worst excesses of political correctness. But sometimes it only delays their impact. And perhaps it is apt that P.C. stands also for police constable.

The state, as much in New Zealand as elsewhere, or more, has pulled back behind some of its frontiers. It has advanced beyond others and the nopersonsland it has left has been filled. These are years and this is the land, in which we are told what to do, rather than encouraged to make a choice. Kiwis are governed still, but still not by themselves.

Of Communication and Courtesy

In Britain you are always thanking and being thanked. Thanks ever so, indeed. Kiwis use the words less, but perhaps mean them more. Not that it is common in either country to show too much emotion. The stiff upper lip exists in the South Pacific as well as the North Atlantic.

The telephone prevails. Writing letters is not popular either as a pastime or as a mode of conducting business. Even addressing government departments by letter will often produce a telephone call in response. Perhaps you are flattered to think that it shows a personal touch. Then you find yourself writing down their verbal reply as if you were the secretary. And you realise that they

can still say you got it wrong, whereas they would be committed by a written statement.

Charging for local calls, you might think, would limit the practice. So it may, but it has only recently been introduced and it does not apply to individual subscribers. The answerphone has, of course, taken hold. It is ideal: it seems efficient and modern; it gives the impression you are outdoors (out, anyway, so it helps the burglars). It is often difficult to recognise the occasions on which a live voice is answering. No doubt the next refinement will be the answerphone that expresses surprise when you ask if it is a real person talking. That will confuse the burglars for a while.

If letters are rarely written, e-mail has proved seductive. And Kiwis are careering down the information superhighway as erratically as down any other. Every farmyard has its Gates. And printed material abounds. Junk mail predominates, brought not only by the postpersons (usually female on bikes, in shorts), but by specialists (any sex, any age) in junk mail delivery who bring the rival supermarkets' weekly cut-out coupons, the offer from the man who wants to mow your lawn or paint your iron roof or sell your house for you (or over you).

There are give-away newspapers, paid for by the advertisements with which they are crammed; newsletters from your local authority, from an array of churches and religious organisations, from the Lions and the Scouts. And it is all at the front gate (if there is one), where the letter box stands: not a hole in the front door, as in Britain, but a free-standing structure whose contents indicate whether you are out, away or still in bed.

And there will be a few callers, too. Charities will call on Saturday mornings or Monday nights (and leave an envelope if you are out). Plastic bags will be left for discarded clothing. And an annual telethon combines charity, TV addiction and telephone mania.

The social call is relatively rare, perhaps because the cities are large and the country population sparse. Invitations are, happily, much less rare. Dining out at a restaurant has become more common, especially, but not only, among the expense account classes. Invitations to a domestic lunch or dinner are not infrequent, however, though it is likely that your host or hostess will be doing all the work. You take them a bottle of wine, a bunch of flowers or a box of chocolates.

The emphasis on the outdoors may mean your invitation will be to a barbecue or sausage sizzle (but not a clambake). There the male of the family is more likely to be in charge, probably aproned, a poor beforked thing, and making a good job of steaks and satays. He may prefer real wood and charcoal. Or he may use gas or electricity.

The drawback to these occasions is the noise. Outdoor parties too often are accompanied by the stereo. Even indoor parties tend to become loud. Sometimes the neighbours are invited, as a way of warning them, or securing insulation from their complaints. Certainly no insulation can prevail against the relentless beat of amplified rock without which, unfortunately, a Kiwi party is rarely complete. There is no sense that this is

aural pollution, no sense that it invades others' privacy.

Maybe the young are the worst offenders. Sometimes their parties – allegedly joined by 'free-loaders' or uninvited guests – spread across the street. Occasionally the police are called in.

Sending an invitation can cause a problem. Is the couple married? Does she prefer to use her maiden name if she is married? The Kiwi practice is to send the invitation to 'X and partner'. This, of course, offends virtually everyone: those without a partner at all; and those with a partner to whom they are married; and those partners who would like to have a name of their own. The straight see it as a suggestion that they might be gay and the gay as an indication of ignorance. So it is: but the attempt to redeem it may be considered undue curiosity.

The phone may again help. Again you will not have to commit yourself so plainly. Do bring Jack/Jill, too, won't you? There is still the risk that Jack or Jill are over the hill.

Greetings come in various forms. Sir and Madam are rarely used. Mate is rarer than in Australia, Sir much rarer than in the U.K. Good day is as common as Good morning, if not more so. Americanisms creep in: Hi! Or Australianisms: How are yer? How would you be? How're you doing? On the phone the quizzical 'Are you there?' seems to have died out with the advance in telecom technology. Kia ora! is for the bicultured.

Farewells include the normal goodbye. There are other variants. 'Hooray!' supplements 'cheers'. 'See you' is often used, even though the chances of so doing may be remote, or not particularly to be looked forward to. Anything is surely better than Americanisms like 'There you go'. Or, worse still, 'Have a good day', which can still be delivered at you at 5.00 p.m. when your day has already proved awful and the evening promises no better.

Shaking hands more or less follows the British pattern: a common practice, but often with a touch of hesitation and not repeated too often. The same applies to the greeting kiss. Hugs are rare. Soccer is, after all, not the national game.

Old-fashioned courtesies are, in New Zealand as in Britain, just that. Doors may be held open; men may rise as other guests come or go. But giving up a seat on a bus is improbable (though children can get a cheaper seat in Wellington if they undertake to do it when the bus is full). The worst manners are those of car drivers.

Foreign languages are admired, but not much learned. In a country with so much international trade and so many international travellers, the lack of interest is surprising. Moreover, the Kiwis exaggerate the extent to which knowledge of a foreign language conveys an understanding of a foreign culture. The difficulty found in pursuing the former, which is exaggerated, means that the latter is seen as impractical also.

If foreign languages are kept at arm's length, English is manhandled. When Strine was analysed, an attempt was made to analyse New Zild. The accent is not like the Australian, still less like the Cockney, which Australian is sometimes mistakenly said to resemble. It has neither the glottal stop of London, nor the dark L,

nor the upper-class-lah for ly ('reallah' for really). Characteristic is an upward inflection at the end of a sentence. Statements tend to sound like questions, as if seeking confirmation. 'Eh?' often ends a sentence.

In neither Australia nor New Zealand is there the regional variation characteristic of Britain itself. In the deep South, however, you will hear a rich rolled R attributed, like Dunedin's interest in whisky and education, to Scottish immigration.

Teaching Kiwis to speak proper is no longer seen as the proper task of speech teachers: a good, rather neutral, Kiwi mode of speech is the objective. The main challenges are flattened vowels and lack of consonants.

Kiwis are devoted, not only to committees, but to speeches. Almost any occasion is the occasion for a speech. Yet, except for Maori, they speak as if unaccustomed to public speaking. Make for a chair if the exhibition opening or the staff farewelling takes this turn, as it is sure to do. You may be in for what Evelyn Waugh described in Lord Copper's case as a 'tropic tide of oratory'. The experienced know the signals. One is the emergence of a folder of notes from a pocket or a handbag and potential listeners nervously try to count the number of pages the speaker is turning over. Worse still are those who think they can speak without notes. In this volcanic land the supply of natural gas is unlimited. Mrs Malaprop would rightly 'reprehend' the 'derangement of epitaphs' that results.

The written language has suffered in New Zealand as elsewhere. Apostrophes are like hundreds and thousands on a child's dessert, sprinkled at random.

The use of the plural is singular. 'Smoking and eating is prohibited' the notices at The University of Auckland enjoin.

Maori is an official language, too. Pakeha New Zealanders rarely learn it, even though it is not foreign. Official New Zealand makes some recognition of it: public institutions and state-owned enterprises have acquired Maori names as well as English ones. Pakeha public speakers often begin with (lamentably pronounced) Maori greetings.

For the Maori their language is a treasure (taonga). Maori leaders are anxious to ensure that it remains a live language and they bestow on it a care that Kiwi English language hardly gets, except in dictionaries. And the Maori have a great tradition of oratory, which, unlike the Pakeha, they honour in the observance rather than the breach.

The English idiom is rich in words of assurance: 'She'll be right.' 'Good on you.' 'She's apples, mate.' Swearing, however, is more notable for quantity than variety. The two four-letter words are ubiquitous.

[illegible] of the plural is singular: 'Some sheep.' [illegible] predictable [illegible] at [illegible] [illegible] with.

[illegible] is [illegible] ideology [illegible] Pakeha. New [illegible] leaders [illegible], even though it is not [illegible] of New Zealand makes some recognition [illegible] public institutions and state-owned [illegible] have [illegible] Maori names as well as English [illegible] Pakeha public speakers often begin with [illegible] in Maori greetings.

For the Maori their language [illegible] leaders [illegible] anxious to [illegible] language and they [illegible] are that Eng[lish] [illegible] language [illegible] [illegible] dictionary. And the Maori have a great tradition of [illegible] unlike the Pakeha, they honour [illegible] rather than the breath.

The English [illegible] rich [illegible] of [illegible] [illegible] [illegible] [illegible] apples, make [illegible] more [illegible] for [illegible] variety. The two four-letter words are ubiquitous.

Of Cultures and Migrations

Culture means many things to many people. Depending on the definition, it means nothing to some. It can be high, it can be pop; it can be élite, it can be mass. Sometimes it is a word of admiration or a mode of justification. It is a way of signalling difference, often standing in for something less acceptable, like race. It is also a way of indicating what is shared.

Apply one meaning to New Zealand and you will find a high culture that is 'Western', reflecting the inheritance of Britain and the contact with it, but also the impact of the U.S. and of Australia.

Although many Continental Europeans have to come to New Zealand, they have made less of a mark than the post-war influx into Australia. Some of them, like the Dutch, indeed prided themselves on their ability to

assimilate. There were fewer Italians and Greeks. The big New Zealand cities have a less European air than those in Australia: they are less American, too, perhaps as a result. But visitors could never think they were in an English city.

By contrast, the cities, particularly Auckland, but not Auckland alone, contain other communities, Maori, who increasingly left the countryside in the 1950s and 1960s, Samoans, Tongans, Niueans and Cook Islanders who came in search of better wages in the 1960s and 1970s.

Asian migration into Australia and New Zealand, much restricted from the late nineteenth century, has increased, particularly in the last decade or so. Chinese from Taiwan, Hong Kong and Malaysia have made their homes in New Zealand, adding to the rather small numbers of Laotians and Khmers who came, mostly as refugees, in the 1970s and the Indians who left Fiji after Colonel Rabuka's coups in the 1980s, and a rapidly growing Korean community.

Western culture in New Zealand is fragmented in more than one way. As elsewhere, there is a gulf between the élite and the pop. That does not stop members of the élite savouring the pop, even taking it seriously, sometimes over-seriously. Nor does it altogether stop the reverse process, though more inhibitions stand in the way. Commercialism does not necessarily hinder it: British Airways can use a tune from an anti-British opera. It is possible that an opera star can prompt those who believed they did not like opera to try it out. In a small country like New Zealand, the sense of national pride in a singer like Kiri Te Kanawa may help to bring élite and mass together. The same may be true of other achievements that the whole country can celebrate: in rugby, in round-the-world yachting, though watching that has been compared to watching paint dry. And it was a Kiwi who, with Sherpa Tensing, got to the top of Everest first.

O.E.

Small countries like New Zealand run the risk of being culturally submerged. The risk was always there. It has, perhaps, increased with the advent of satellite TV. But that only follows on the impact of the movie, the video and the airport paperback.

In the late nineteenth century the Kiwi, élite and otherwise, reacted by an assertive imperialism: they were British, but rather better British than the British

themselves. Lonely and remote, they were dependent, but wanted to be distinctive. And not only would they play a role on Britain's imperial stage; they could have their own empire in the South Pacific.

A different kind of nationalism sought to make New Zealand culture distinctive in a more distinctive way. That concern was, for example, felt by the intellectuals of the depression and post-war years. Was there a distinctive voice in New Zealand literature or New Zealand music? It was not confined to the intellectuals, however. The Lilburn symphonies co-existed with Split Enz.

What was clearly distinctive was the possession of Maori culture. Whose possession was it, however? Clearly it was the possession, first of all, of the Maori people. They had fought the wars with the settlers with courage and resource, but at the end of the last century, when social Darwinism prevailed, they were thought to be a dying race. Certainly their culture was undervalued. The official aim was assimilation.

They survived even so. The political system gave them some opportunities and they produced some remarkable leaders. They played a distinguished role in the two world wars in which New Zealand participated so boldly. What became important for them, as they moved into the towns, was to take a fuller role in the professions, in education and government. At the same time, Maori traditions could be reasserted or built upon as a spur to such an endeavour. It did not need imported biculturalism to send New Zealand society down this track, though its signposting helped.

Maori assertiveness

Where the track leads is still not clear. Maori and Pakeha live together and indeed are much intermarried. How will they preserve and develop their 'cultures'? The Maori tradition helps to make New Zealand distinctive. But borrowing it only as the trappings of an essentially monocultural society will no longer be acceptable. It will savour of tokenism and paternalism. Logos are not enough.

If, however, Maori culture must thrive, so must New Zealand as a whole. It needs to use all its resources and all its talents for the benefit of all. Divisiveness is sterile. So, perhaps, is an overdose of sensitivity. 'Cultural safety' could be dangerous.

Such an accommodation has to take account as well of the cultures of the Pacific Island (or Polynesian) peoples who have made New Zealand their home or their home from home. They are, of course, themselves distinctive and sometimes at odds – do not lump them together as Islanders.

There is a risk, too, that recent Asian immigrants will be set apart, even seen with envy or malice. Most of the Khmer and Vietnamese came in poverty and attracted sympathy. But some have done well, spurred by the determination immigrants often show, and even the relaxed Kiwi may find it difficult to accept that a place in the Medical School is denied their kid by a high-achiever of Asian origin.

Recent migrants have often been wealthier. Indeed the 1980s migration programme was designed to attract, initially as PRs (Permanent Residents), the skills and wealth of those who had made so much of the opportunities of Hong Kong and Taiwan, the future of which now seems uncertain. That wealth can be a source of envy, too. Driving to school in a Mercedes is not a very sensible way of avoiding it, and ethnic jealousies often begin among adolescents.

Not much thought has gone into the migration programme, still less into its administration, though commission seekers have made some money out of it (and so have real estate agents). Grandma is left to look after the kids and she knows no English. And they may not know much either.

Not only is there a risk of racialism. Positive cultural benefits tend to be lost. Even a 'market-driven' ideology could recognise some of them. The special skills of the immigrants are hardly turned to sufficient account.

New Zealand has been populated by a series of migrations. That has often meant conflict. But it has also meant something positive. Tolerance keeps breaking out.

Of Food and Drink

The real Kiwi eats tofu, dusted with wheatgerm, topped with sultanas. That recent report related to the bird itself kept in a zoo, it turned out. But the human Kiwi has gone 'up-market', too.

New Zealanders' eating habits have indeed been transformed in the past 20 years. Something like that has happened elsewhere too, and for some of the same reasons. Prosperity is one and uncertainty about its continuance another. Tomorrow we may not die, but the stockmarket will probably collapse.

International travel is yet another. There is still, of course, a tendency to avoid foreign foods when in foreign parts: for the Japanese to seek a sushi bar in Auckland and for the British to forage for fish and chips in Spain

(and to ask for bacon and eggs in the Middle East). Maybe the tendency will disappear when all the world eats Kentucky Fried Chicken (now made healthy by abbreviation to KFC). And so we should indeed eat and drink (and be merry), for tomorrow we may not have any choice.

Travel broadens the appetite. Kiwis are travellers and may have brought back tastes and skills acquired in their overseas experience. Migrants, too, have been emboldened to diversify our diet. Though not to the extent of Melbourne and Sydney – which perhaps provide the world's best dining – the New Zealand cities offer a richness and diversity in cuisine not offered in other parts of their culture. In my house are many kitchens. The à la carte menu has grown and the table d'hote shrunk.

In the 1960s, restaurants that offered other than the basic diet were few and far between, even in Auckland and Wellington, the commercial and political capitals. That basic diet was not bad, but it was unvarying. It was an antipodean Anglo-Irish menu, quite often prepared by Greeks. Steaks and roasts predominated, with plenty of tomato sauce and bread-and-butter and no salad (and perhaps served on a formica table). The materials were good: what was done to them seldom made them better.

By the 1990s, restaurants had increased in number perhaps 50-fold, even 100-fold. And like the states in the UN, they became not only more numerous, but more various (and perhaps of less certain durability). Indeed they increasingly represented a UN, often specialising in the food of a particular country or a region in it. The ingredients remained good. New Zealand restaurants combined that with a level of skill and preparation hitherto unimagined. If Cook discovered New Zealand, New Zealand has now discovered the chef.

Kiwi cuisine

At times there has been a sense of overkill, if not a clear threat to health. Menus became descriptive, if hardly analytical, as if it were necessary to educate the eater. Or maybe it is a way of insisting on the cleverness of the chef, rather as producers of plays and operas try to point out in the programme the intelligence of their work and the wide range of their imagination and erudition, instead of leaving the proof of the pudding where it should be. A characteristic feature is the blackboard menu. Then the waiter or waitress (more often the latter) explains – perhaps again with a touch of the school monitor – the compilation of the chef's specials, what has been done by way of cauli or coulis, whether the camembert has been (blasphemously) fried.

For the most part you will indeed be well waited-upon, usually by young people, since the industry is itself young. Sometimes they will be part-time workers, students, for example. You will not get water American-style: you will have to ask for it. You will get bread. And of bread too, New Zealand now offers a wonderful variety. You could live by it alone.

Will you get wine? Until the 1960s, alcohol was available with food only if you were a bona fide traveller staying in a licensed hotel and not available after 6.00 p.m. except with food. A national referendum then asked two questions: should New Zealand's Parliament have a four-year term instead of a three-year one? Should six o'clock closing cease? The pundits expected a yes vote to the first and no to the second. As, happily, they often are, the pundits were wrong. A more civilised kind of drinking followed: you no longer had to swill it down between finishing work and going home to 'tea' (dinner). And the restaurants that were emerging were licensed to sell wine with their food.

There was one helpful carry-over (or hangover). Those who had drunk alcohol while eating their food in a restaurant had brought bottles in, sometimes wrapped in newspaper and, once opened, kept out of sight, perhaps rather ostentatiously: the risk added to the relish. The custom of bringing wine in remained, though now there was no need to disguise it. Most restaurants allow customers to bring their own wine, even some of those that mark up their own wine list in a manner that readily emulates that of the old world.

BYO is the acronym: bring your own (sometimes BYOG – Bring Your Own Grog). Taking your drink into an eating-place became common. So, curiously enough, did taking your food out of it, known in New Zealand as 'takeaways'. The Chinese were, perhaps, the first in the field. Franchise-holders of the American brands followed. And now you do not even have to take away: there are pizza couriers.

And what else might you find at home? Ready-made dinners, frozen or thawed, though not in the variety that Marks and Spencer offer. And of course, home-cooking, itself more inventive and as always, if successful, unsurpassable.

The ingredients remain good. Some of the best stuff, no doubt, is exported, or is priced as if it were being re-imported from Japan. Fish, a particular focus for the Japanese, is particularly dear, though usually superb. Venison is less deer: previously hunted by helicopter, now farmed (and marketed, incomprehensibly, as cervena). Chicken is common, duck rarer, goose almost non-existent.

Fruit is of varying quality and somewhat seasonal. Apples and apricots, plums and cherries, do well in the south; strawberries, citrus and melons, in the north; berryfruits somewhere in between. Not even the north is tropical enough for papaya and pineapple and banana. The kiwifruit is a triumph of marketing as well as horticulture. Previously the humble Chinese gooseberry, it was renamed. But its success led others to follow. The fruit now seems to be in permanent world glut. Other attempts to domesticate exotic fruit and then re-export it have not succeeded.

It is best with a pav. This is short for pavlova, a meringue-based dish which is claimed by some as the national dish but blamed by others on the Australians.

Leave room for it after the deep fried camembert for starters and the pan-fried hoki for entrée and the garlic bread and the venison steak.

There are other ways of making up a menu. An extreme form of à la carte might be called 'table de guest'. In New Zealand this is called 'Ladies a plate'. Found on or spoken during an invitation, these words invite the guests to contribute food to the party. Not merely BYOG. Unsuspecting Poms (English people) have been known to bring the plate alone, as if crockery were rarely used. The result can be a testimony of skill and imagination. It can also be humiliating. Will all your asparagus rolls or rumballs be still on your plate when the time comes to wash up and go home?

Watch out for the (variously-spelled) smorgasbord. This combines table d'hôte and à la carte. Once common in New Zealand, it appears to have had its heart eaten out. No one, even in a land of plenty, could resist piling their plate high and returning for 'seconds' and 'sweets'.

'Half-cut' means tiddly and 'grog' means alcohol. Increasingly it means wine. Beer, actively promoted, is, despite the 'wowsers', widely drunk, cold, delivered by bottle, by can, or by hose. Wine was formerly called 'plonk', or, because immigrants from Dalmatia were among the earlier winemakers, 'Dally plonk', but no longer. Quality and variety are again of a different order compared with what was produced even in the 1960s. Different varieties have been tried; and areas hitherto not thought suitable, like Marlborough, even Central Otago ('Central'), have been planted. New Zealand Chardonnays lead the new world, if not the old as well. But you can find some nice reds, too, again using the grape for their name, pinot or cabernet (since the French have reserved their claims to claret and burgundy), and often adding the name of a real or virtually real vineyard with an environmentally cosy aroma (Muddy Creek, Narrow Neck Estate, Waikaremoana Red, etc.).

One result has, of course, been to open up a new world to wine snobbery and to its extraordinary literature that insists on invoking the taste of other fruits to describe it, but that, like other snobberies, has a nice little line in put-down words.

The old plonk still exists. Some of it now in 'casks' – plastic bags in cardboard boxes ('chateau cardboard' to some) – but its quality may surpass the standards of an earlier generation. You will probably not find a really good sherry and you should probably avoid liqueurs, even (or especially) kiwifruit. Mead has not caught on.

But New Zealand honey is itself one of the wonders of the world, fragrant with its native flora, rata, pohutukawa. You are not allowed to take it into Australia: its honey cannot compete.

Coming to New Zealand, you are allowed to bring in duty-free no fewer than six bottles of wine. That shows a justified confidence in the local product. It's not cheap, but it's worth more than you pay. Have a glass or two now and you will think the same of this book.

Of Recreation and Relaxation

Leisure and pleasure are not the same thing. The former may lead to the latter, but sometimes the connection is remote, even perverse and of limited duration.

Jogging is a case in point. It is a leisure-time activity for many (although not perhaps for those who start at 5.30 a.m.). It can often lead, in turn, to short-term pain, as breath as well as body comes in short pants, as the fitter pass the fatter and the younger the older who have only their stamina to console them; to middle-term pleasure, as you realise you have survived and you can settle to a few beers and tucker or kai (food) with a clear conscience; and to long-term pain, as arthritis takes hold and the effect of incessant pounding belatedly rebounds.

The Kiwis are great joggers. It seems that they also invented the oxymoronic (or maybe merely moronic) 'fun-run'. In this, thousands of citizens (and PRs) run, walk, jog several kilometres, hosed down at intervals by the occupants of the houses they pass. Sometimes they even pay for the privilege of being involved. The pleasure lies in the achievement and perhaps in the sense of togetherness: a curious mix, once more, of competition and community. 'No sweat' is a Kiwi phrase for easily done: it does not apply to a fun run.

The Sportsman

Exercise is certainly a common Kiwi way of filling leisure hours. Some of it is very exacting, the triathlon for example; some insane, like bungy jumping (at $500 a go). Every kind of sport is attempted, from hang-gliding to bowls, from skiing to surfing, from tae kwon do to billiards, from tramping to trampolining, from white-water rafting to wrestling, from abseiling sky-scrapers to octopush. Boats have overtaken horses as the resort of the wealthy.

Leisure can be filled with mere games, some active, some passive. The national game is rugby. But every kind of game is played by amateurs, professionals or both, from scrabble to soccer, from petanque to patience, from bridge to basketball. Here the Kiwis have not been inventive. There seem to be no native Kiwi games, not even of the doubtful quality of Aussie rules. But they like to make a game of it. Couriers really run. Theatresports is the most popular kind of drama. And house painters cannot work without the radio on 'full bore'.

Golf is an inexpensive game in New Zealand. The clubhouse retains its attraction, even though licensed drinking is now more freely available. The same is true of bowls, a favoured game. Casinos have recently been introduced, first in reputedly respectable Christchurch, now in a vast building in not even reputedly respectable Auckland. But the gambler already had plenty of scope at the TAB or with Lotto.

Bush walking is freely available, but it is not to be attempted, as too often it is, by the unwary or the unprepared. The bush, like the coast, looks less

frightening than it is. It is thick, easy to get lost in, an uncertain friend even to its familiars.

New Zealanders probably treat their sea with insufficient caution too. Going fishing is a favourite leisure activity and not merely a metaphor for knocking off. But fishermen are not always as wise as they are wishful. They will go out in small boats when a high wind is raging or stand on slippery rocks when a big surf is up.

Just going to the beach has its dangers, too. The surf itself, frightening on occasion, can also be treacherous. Body-surfing, board-surfing and wind-surfing require skill and nerve and – often less available – common sense. Surf lifesavers are on duty much of the summer. Mostly young, not all men, they indulge a leisure-time activity that is essential to others' enjoyment. There are still those who risk their lives as well as those of the lifesavers by swimming 'outside the flags'.

There are man-made menaces, too, besides the sea (and the sandflies). More environment-conscious than a decade or so ago, the Kiwis will still strew glass bottles and plastic bags and soft drink cans and pizza boxes along the extraordinarily beautiful coastline of their islands. 'Boaties' used indeed to believe that if you broke bottles before throwing them overboard, the action of the waves would blunt the edges of the glass. They were often wrong, as paddlers found.

You will not find deck chairs on the beach (nor, except for rare migrants, men with rolled up trousers and newspaper hats). You will find the chillybin. And you will be bothered by the transistor and the ghetto-blaster, sometimes belting its heartlessness out when the owner has in fact escaped into the sea.

You are more likely to find the sun than on an English beach. It is also more likely to burn you. Increasingly Kiwis are taking again to hats and caps, as the risks of melanoma are recognised. The fresh complexioned English sun-seeker should be cautious. But it is the Kiwis who spent their holidays in the Kiwi sun as kids who are most affected.

If exercise is not necessarily leisure and not always pleasure, there are other ways of filling the hours away from work that are as equivocal. One, of course, is work itself. 'The garden is a loathsome thing', Sellars and Yeatman rightly declared: but for some it is lovesome. A love-hate relationship is indeed common. Remember that in large parts of New Zealand the winter is mild. The garden hardly ceases to grow. And you can year-round enjoy disturbing your neighbour by motormowing before breakfast as well as chainsawing on otherwise somnolent Sunday afternoons and weedeating weekday evenings. Maybe, drawing on the colonial past, you can enjoy beating back the fast-growing plants your predecessors so mistakenly introduced.

D.I.Y. is also a pleasure for some, if not a necessity. Kiwis are often unusually skilled in carpentry, drain-digging, mechanical repairs, house-painting, not as a result of formal training but, it seems, as a result of learning from dad. Neighbours, though they may be inclined quietly to scoff, are likely also actively to help.

Pleasure is to be found in less active pursuits. Kiwis are said to buy and borrow an unusually large number

of books. The number of books published in New Zealand is certainly strikingly large, although, of course, most of what is read comes from the U.K. and the U.S. The bookshops are rarely well stocked. You may have to wait for a title to be ordered (or 'indented') from 'overseas' and then you will have to be propped up when you hear how the price has been 'marked up'. You may have to indent recorded music. Only one or two shops keep a stock that exceeds 10,000 items. But they are run by people who know and care. And the 'mark-up' is far less.

You can escape advertising on the radio (there is a 'Third-Programme' channel, Concert FM), but not on TV. There it has in fact reached saturation or beyond. Programmes are butchered to find space for it. David Lawrence, a critic, calls it 'an insult – excessive even in comparison to some American commercial channels'.

You can pursue every kind of hobby as well as every kind of sport. If you are a collector, your scope may be limited and the dealers will be aware of international prices. What is now an antique, of course, is, in New Zealand as elsewhere, something merely pre-post-modern: something worn or used not by grandma, but by mother.

'One reassuring thing about modern art is that things can't be as bad as they are painted', Walthall Jackson said. Collect New Zealand paintings from one of the many dealer galleries; collect New Zealand pottery, watching for work influenced but not overwhelmed by Japanese practice; collect New Zealand wines, too, not merely for their investment value. But beware of the wine at exhibition openings.

Music is probably the most well-supported of the arts in New Zealand. New Zealand rock can be distinguished, at least by experts, from the imported variety; but young Kiwis are as obsessed as any by the international stars, ephemeral or otherwise. Musicals are extraordinarily popular, not only because of the international promotion they receive. Kiwis are brought up with them. A secondary school's major artistic endeavour for the year may be to produce a musical.

The conservatoria or schools of music attached to several universities and to the Wellington Polytechnic produce music as well as musicians. The New Zealand Symphony is widely held to be the best orchestra south of the equator, not only by Kiwis, and it has made some of the best Naxos discs. Chamber music, devotees of which were increased when refugees came from Central Europe in the 1930s, has never lost its hold, while opera, popular in the colonial New Zealand of the later nineteenth century, is regaining its position in the late twentieth, with New Zealand productions that rival the quality and sophistication of those in other parts of the world in ways that the enterprising old antipodean travelling companies could not. The latest fashion is open-air concerts, concluding with the *1812* overture.

Straight plays are less sure of an audience. Roger Hall has succeeded as a Kiwi Ayckbourn. Sinclair and McCarten found it difficult to repeat the success of *Ladies Night*. Auckland has lost its full-time professional theatre, but Wellington has two.

Sometimes it seems, of course, that the interval (not intermission) is the most important part of play or concert or opera. Not only can you (now) have a drink. You can see your friends (and enemies). And in New Zealand the same people turn up each time.

The arts are not highly subsidised. What the Arts Council, now tastelessly renamed Creative New Zealand (are they all accountants?) distributes comes partly from government, partly from the Lottery Grants Board. Some arts organisations see its distribution as a lottery, too.

Keeping arts magazines going is difficult in a small market. *Landfall*, a literary journal, is the most distinguished. The more widely-read *New Zealand Listener*, a kind of a radio-TV times, has lost some of its audience and some of its range.

'Neat' is a word of praise in New Zealand (sometimes equated to 'good', 'good one'). The countryside is not, like Britain's, neat: it is often rather ragged. The city streets are a tangle of overhead wires: power lines as well as phone lines are generally above ground. There are some nice houses (usually bungalows, but not called that); there is no great building. People live in houses (rather than flats or home units) surrounded by their garden (section), though there is a trend towards 'in-fill' (another house in what was the garden). Houses are not named: the 'Mon Repos' of England or the 'Avacoola' of Australia do not exist. Maybe they are loved. But the average Kiwi moves a lot.

New Zealand films are marked by Kiwi eccentricity. Kiwi violence, too: is it an assertion that it is an interesting place after all? *The Piano* was much admired, despite its playing to the gallery. Go to Kare Kare beach, near Auckland, if you are a devotee. That was the real thing about it.

Of Sickness and Health

New Zealanders do not generally offer the toast 'Good health'. But the subject is frequently on their lips. Indeed Aotearoa might be renamed Hypochondria.

No doubt the colonial phase offered plenty of life-threatening challenges, apart from the Anglo-Maori wars. They were, however, not of the same order as in tropical territories. There are mosquitoes but no malaria. There are no big cats. Indeed there are scarcely any native mammals at all; no snakes, although they are one of the Kiwi phobias. Fauna indeed are extra-ordinarily non-threatening in New Zealand: only the weta, hanging in drawn curtains, may alarm, by surprise more than menace. Man, however, introduced new

diseases, as well as new plants and animals, and new medicines and methods had to follow.

In New Zealand, as in Australia, doctors enjoy a social prestige and often, not always, an income to match. Getting into the medical schools attached to two of the universities is extremely competitive. Medical matters are highly newsworthy and medical research attracts ready financial support.

The state has played a large role in providing medical care particularly since the first Labour government in the 1930s. Its relationship with the doctors has been a mixture of co-operation and contention. What should the state provide? What is the role of the private sector? How should doctors be remunerated? How much should the patient pay for a visit or prescription or operation?

The government has also begun to argue with itself. The fourth Labour government and its successors adopted a right-wing ideology. The aim was not only to economise but to make people value services financially. Hospitals are now called Crown Health Enterprises. New Zealanders have been inventive in this sphere as in others. Plunket nursing was their contribution to early twentieth century baby care (and mother cowing). But the new venture is surely more problematic. 'The country's health system emerges from major surgery', says the *New Zealand Herald*, 'although restrictions on the public knowing the condition of the patient make it difficult to judge whether the operation has been successful or whether post-operative shock has set in.' Perhaps it is just as well that on the whole New Zealand is a healthy place. There are plenty of 'wogs' (germs, bugs), but Kiwis are seldom really 'crook' (sick, ill).

At the same time as the government took steps towards 'deregulation' and 'competition' in health 'provision', it also became more interventionist in regulating personal hygiene. Preventive medicine is indeed as important as curative, no doubt. But the restless desire to regulate is as important a motive. Perhaps even more than most, Kiwis like telling each other what to do. Perhaps, worse still, they like being told. But they are not alone in the rectification campaigns that, dying out in post-Mao China, have spread into the post-industrial world. Is it a plague?

No doubt smoking is harmful to health and not only the health of the smoker. But the methods for dealing with it abandoned education for intrusion. Is it surprising that New Zealand leaders have often expressed admiration for Lee Kuan Yew, statesman of Singapore, grandmother of all granny states? The young, especially women, especially Maori women, smoke as a kind of protest.

Dentists, never part of the national health scheme, are paid even better than doctors; but they now have less to do as a result of the fluoridation of the water supply. That provoked public discussion as an undesirable interference with liberty a generation ago. New Zealanders have moved on since then. Or back? Perhaps the price is high after all.

Public hygiene indeed leaves something to be desired. The water supply, fluoridation apart, is not always above suspicion: the chlorine is often obvious. Sometimes you may be better off at the bach, collecting rain water off

the roof. Only recently have the larger cities brought their sewage more or less under control. You may no longer recall Prince Charles's comment on swimming off a Melbourne beach. 'Just going through the motions', he said. Aucklanders, however, have been warned not to swim after heavy rain. Down at the bach, you will be relying, however, on a septic tank, or even a hole in the ground. It's as well the water comes off the roof.

Personal hygiene recalls English weather rather than English practice: frequent showers rather than weekly baths.

Canine hygiene, as in England, leaves something to be desired. Joggers and beach-lovers need to be cautious. There are regulations against polluting the footpath (not pavement, nor sidewalk) and against exercising on the beach between dawn and dusk. Maybe dogs just don't read and Kiwis indulge them, almost as much as the English do. Some, however, gamely follow their faecal fauna with the New Zealand version of a pooper-scooper (a supermarket plastic bag). And Kiwis are as mad about cats as the ancient Egyptians: there are 560,000 cats in Auckland, a city of a million humans.

Health enters into the craze for sport. The connection is equivocal. Overdoing the latter prejudices the former, just as underdoing it does. Jogging, even on hard surfaces, remains popular all the same. Jazzercise is popular, too, combining the love of noise with the love of activity (and of wearing the right gear). Maybe it has some effect. To their surprise Aucklanders on average were found in a recent survey to be unusually slim. Cue for a celebratory feast. You will see some hefty people around, Pakeha (European), Maori, Tongan or Samoan, but they will rarely be fat or undignified.

Arthritis and cancer are the ills that beset Kiwis. As elsewhere in the West, the women outlive the men. Those who move into a retirement village or a home (the word is still used) may be exploited as elsewhere. But the best of them provide the best of care. Politically, too, Greypower has made itself felt. But in the view of government, superannuitants have what it takes.

Not that New Zealand has abandoned ageism: compulsory retirement is still in effect. It has, however, gone through the sanitisation of the language that the Americans began, although it has not (yet) taken it to the extremes they have. But our committees are convened by chairpersons and reporters need to be culturally sensitive. A healthy mindlessness in a healthy body.

The hot pools of igneous New Zealand were in colonial times valued like the spas of Europe. Although some of the steam has been taken out of Rotorua in order to heat its homes and hotels, it is still worth trying. Glorious mud.

people around, (whether European, Māori, Tongan or Samoan), but they will [illegible] be [illegible] or undignified.

[illegible] Authority and power are the [illegible] that [illegible] Kiwis. As [illegible] in the West, the [illegible] the men. [illegible] now, in a [illegible] village or a [illegible] word is [illegible] as elsewhere [illegible] Politically [illegible] is the [illegible] of [illegible] takes.

Not that [illegible] agenda [illegible] however, [illegible] through the [illegible] of the language that the [illegible] has not (yet) taken it to the [illegible] they have. But our committees are convened [illegible] and reporters need to be culturally [illegible]. A healthy [illegible] in a healthy body.

[illegible] New Zealand were [illegible] [illegible] Although [illegible] to [illegible] homes and hotels, it is still worth [illegible].

eight

Of Drivers

'Art thou pale for weariness of climbing heaven and gazing on the earth?' That was Shelley's prescient description of jet lag.

International travel seldom shows people at their best. Americans abroad are more imperious, Britons more supercilious, Australians more vulgar. The Kiwi, however, travels well. The chief threat is to other Kiwis living overseas. At the slightest hint of an invitation, the visitors will stay for a week or a month, 'bludging' on their mates. These birds really settle in your nest. The campervan is parked outside and O.E. extended.

Domestic travel is another matter. Public transport is relatively safe and the behaviour, even in the last

bus, relatively orderly. Waiting queue-lessly for a taxi, an earlier source of dispute, now seems to be a thing of the past, as taxis have multiplied with deregulation (and consequent unemployment) and 'shuttles' (shared taxis) have been put on the road. There is no underground railway to terrorise. In fact there is not much public transport at all. There are two main airlines, competing, but in fact, as is characteristic of airlines, almost indistinguishable, much used between the main centres and grudgingly calling at other destinations: they have a good safety record (any pilot who can land at Rongotai on a windy Wellington day has passed the supreme test). Railways carry little passenger traffic and suburban services, except in Wellington, are limited. Buses, some run by the railways, are cheaper.

The private car, however, is the main means of conveyance. Car ownership is at a high level (and cars, unlike houses, are often named: you can buy 'personalised' registration plates, limited to six letters and/or figures). Not many cars are now put together in New Zealand. Japanese models predominate, sometimes second-hand (indeed more so than their speedometers indicate). But the variety is considerable. So is the age-range.

Do not try, however, to assess the position by observation. In New Zealand you need to keep all your attention, as pedestrian or driver, on the road and in particular on the other occupants of the road. For there the anarchy in the Kiwi prevails over the orderly, and the aggressive over the considerate. Jekyll and Hyde it seemed to a recent Canadian visitor:

The ordinary, pacific, good-humoured New Zealander, when placed in control of a motor vehicle, suddenly develops a leering, maniacal attitude towards his fellows in other vehicles and his patient, courteous manner disappears in a cloud of turbocharged exhaust.

Driving

The eccentricity of the Kiwi driver is encouraged by the eccentricity of the Kiwi traffic regulations. The Kiwis have devised some rules that, if they are not unique, certainly ought to be. Turning left, you must give way to an oncoming driver turning right in front of you. This baffles everyone else on the road. You are supposed to keep to the left, but, where the road has painted white lines, you may also overtake on the left. The result is an amount of weaving that can make your head (and your steering-wheel) spin (but, it is to be hoped, not your car).

The traffic engineers make their contribution, too. Unlike those in Britain, they prefer traffic lights to

roundabouts, but avoid synchronisation. The lights themselves are on various systems. Some promote what was called, after the overseas consultant concerned, the Barnes dance: all traffic stops, and pedestrians may cross diagonally. Others behave differently and are phased so that the pedestrian is conveniently halfway across when traffic approaches from behind. Some lights appear to be regulated by the amount of traffic; others by a whimsical computer (or a bureaucrat, probably having morning tea) in Wellington. The effect is that drivers are either never ready for the change, or try to beat the lights. Some in any case have a perverse delight in starting off slowly when the light goes green. That can afford the pleasure of stranding the next cars in the line until the next change.

The engineers have great faith in painting white and yellow lines and arrows, but that faith, like others, is widely seen as their own business. They also write on the roads, reading forwards: Child That Mind. Peds should be assumed to mean pedestrians, not pederasts.

Some Kiwis appear to be paralysed by the challenge their fellow-drivers offer them. They conclude that it is best to drive slowly (though not necessarily in the left lane) and to brake a lot (though not necessarily intending to stop). This means that horns are sounded and cars tail each other less than a body apart. Whose body is it anyway?

The car's equipment is used in ways that a visitor will do well to become aware of. A flashing trafficator means: I have just turned. A flashing double-warning light means: I am double-parked and I know it's illegal, but I shouldn't be too long. If you have a car stereo, turn it up so that you cannot hear trains on level crossings or ambulance sirens. When talking to a companion, concentrate on the conversation and keep up eye contact with the passenger to your left rather than the road ahead. If you interrupt the conversation, it should only be in order to curse the old lady in the car in front (too slow) or the bus behind (too close).

Motorways (not freeways, though they are free) exist only near the main centres. The rest of the country has a road network that has to deal, like the railway, with some challenging physical obstacles. Generally it does well, though not as well as the speed of the driving assumes. International signs are used and a few others, too. 'Watch for falling debris' is a confusing instruction. 'Beware of the wind' is good advice.

Accidents are too frequent. The road toll is regularly announced, particularly over the holiday period. The police have been given intrusive powers, to fine on the spot, to stop and administer compulsory breath tests, to use cameras, fixed or mobile (widely seen as revenue-raisers). The Kiwis have only themselves to blame. But it might be well for the police not to concentrate so exclusively on the consumption of alcohol. Better engineering, better regulations, better testing and better education would help.

Be prepared, if you are a newcomer to New Zealand and decide to drive: be prepared for anything. There should be a crash course for visitors.

Be particularly careful if you see a driver wearing a hat: it is doubtful that he knows what he is at. Or she.

Watch for adolescents, to be detected by intertwined bodies, rusting bodywork, the ejection of coca-cola (or even beer) cans at irregular intervals. Watch for the yuppie, using his (usually) cellphone with the other hand lightly on the wheel when not dialling, reading the *Herald* while moving slowly on to the motorway in the rush-hour. Watch for the driver with an arm out of the window for no clear purpose other than aerating the armpit. Watch for the car apparently driven by a large dog from the back seat. Watch, too, for the PR (Permanent Resident). Recent immigrants from the cities of Asia are so amazed at the emptiness of the roads and of the minds of the Kiwi drivers, that they fail to keep their head when all around have clearly lost theirs.

Despite all the signals, formal, or informal (two fingers are in common use), there are Kiwis bold enough to bicycle (helmets are compulsory, even on pushbikes). Some are children at school; others are early workers, keeping fit at the same time. Their daring is coupled with an unjustified reliance on other road-users. They will also mutate into (if not collide into) pedestrians at the traffic lights.

The juggernauts of Europe have not reached New Zealand. But there are some large lorries and they travel as fast and irregularly as any other vehicle. Watch for buses with unexpected acceleration (and, in some cases, of Hungarian provenance, articulated).

It was said of the late and unlamented Kaiser that he treated every day like a Sunday. Perhaps that is the way to describe Kiwi drivers. But what shall we say of them on Sundays?

Words fail us.

Of Law and Enforcement

In New Zealand, as in other Western societies, the definition of crime and the principles of punishment are in contention. But New Zealanders give their own inflection to the argument.

The contention dates back at least to the Enlightenment of the eighteenth century, if not to the end of Eden. Is crime a matter of nature or nurture? How can it be prevented? How can criminals be rehabilitated? What indeed is it? Is it breaching social norms? Is it harming other individuals? Are there crimes against humanity as a whole?

The emphases change over the years. The 1980s – with their endorsement of enterprise, of getting ahead, of rolling back the state (welfare, farewell) – played up

the need for law and order and for the defence of property. At the same time, they promoted white-collar crime, insider-trading, misappropriation and defalcation.

New Zealand took a lead in the changes of the 1980s and shared the drawbacks. Its society did not disintegrate: there were no riots, other than those provoked by the Springbok tour. But burglary became common, security services proliferated and Kiwis became cautious about walking through a park or even about giving a lift to a hitchhiker. It seemed very different from the 1950s, when you could safely leave the front door unlocked when you went out for the day. It was very different from the 1930s, despite the depression that then hit New Zealand rather hard.

The reasons for the contrast, in New Zealand or elsewhere, are not entirely clear. Is it a matter of the breakdown of the family and of the moral guidance it may have given? Does TV offer examples of crime too frequently and too attractively? What is the role of drugs? Certainly New Zealand shares in the drug culture. It is sometimes said to be useful to the international heroin trade because it is relatively open. But those dogs at Auckland's Jean Batten Airport are formidably well-trained, if not thoroughly addicted.

Perhaps the Police – a national force, not a local one – are distracted by other duties, in particular by their campaign to make the roads safer. They are spread thinly in the suburbs. The call to increase the force is a popular one politically. Rolling back the state makes it difficult to achieve.

There are also calls to improve the training of the Police and thus its approach. The officers are polite, if at times supercilious. Are they impartial? Are they understanding? Previously Police and traffic police were separate forces. Recently they have been combined. But the irritation caused by the enforcement of minor traffic punishments is an argument for the former system.

There are other ways in which the system is seen not to be impartial. The force has its Maori members. But Maori form a disproportionate share of the prison population. The Police have a task which New Zealand society itself has to face.

Homosexual acts in private between adults were decriminalised rather belatedly in New Zealand. But maybe, in this and other matters, New Zealanders were ahead of their law-makers. The latter were conscious of the colonial legacy of masculinity, ambiguous though it may have been. They were also exposed to pressure-groups, who sought to impose by government action the values that family and church had once allegedly sustained but now – as they failed to point out – could not sustain.

Censorship is always arbitrary, generally ineffective – the Tsar's government let in *Das Kapital*, but kept out Hobbes' *Leviathan* – and frequently hypocritical. So it is in New Zealand. At a film festival, you can see films you cannot see at other times. But there are attempts to prevent the circulation of video nasties.

Modern technology makes it possible to monitor a society in ways that Stalin could only dream of. New Zealand at least owns up to having a central database

on all its citizens, formerly called the 'Wanganui computer', now moved to a Force 8 earthquake-proof building in an Auckland suburb. It has passed some privacy legislation. But that seems designed to assist government departments to swap information rather than to protect the individual. And if it protects the individual, it seems to do rather better by the guilty than the innocent. It prevents airlines telling you whether the person you are meeting is on the plane. It prevents universities telling their staff which colleagues have been promoted.

Rolling back the state has involved the concept of 'targeting' welfare measures to those who need it and cutting down on the 'dole-bludgers'. That is as intrusive as it is inefficient and it is widely criticised as inhumane. New Zealanders are again at odds with themselves and their concept of the good society.

There is a feeling that the big are punished less than the small. White-collar criminals can have their punishments shortened by good behaviour more easily than others. And they have been known to boast that they can recover their fortunes (though not others').

Lawyers have been tempted by the opportunities of the entrepreneurial 1980s. In New Zealand, moreover, they often act as mortgage agents, investing sums great or small for their clients. At times the trust has been betrayed.

The profession has also become more yuppie. Increasingly organised in recent years into large firms, it is criticised for its profiteering and its neglect of the old values of the family solicitor. Maybe those old virtues were not as solidly based as they seem in retrospect. Maybe, too, the modern criticism is not altogether fair. New Zealand has made a real contribution to the Common Law tradition.

Lawyers have been prominent in politics, the Labour governments of the 1980s included. But the courts showed themselves ready to challenge some of the abuses of power those governments indulged in the name of reform and the free market.

Of Politics and Politicians

Across the Tasman some 18 million people find their governments something of a spectator sport. They have a federal government in Canberra, which is more powerful than the constitution suggests: it has the money. It has six state governments and territorial governments in Canberra and the Northern Territory. Some of the elected parliaments have two houses. There are six Premiers and one Prime Minister. The checks and balances ensure that, even if things are not well considered, they are considered for a long time. Sometimes, like illnesses, they go away. Many governments may in the end govern less.

New Zealand failed to join the federation when it was set up, though a place was left for it. Closer

economic relations in recent years have sometimes suggested that the invitation might be belatedly accepted. It seems unlikely, though New Zealanders characteristically assume that it is only their decision that would count. In many ways, of course, the New Zealand Government is like an Australian State Government. But it has sovereignty and it makes the most of it.

'We are the Gubblement and we mean to gullible this contrary.' These were the words A.R.D. Fairburn ascribed to the Prime Morningstar in the spreach from the prone in 1939. 'Worst of all, I want to comegrabulate the Goddallment on being the boast godallment in the world we live in.'

The government in Wellington is a strong one and its activities closely affect every individual. Intermediate authorities are weak or non-existent. Though reference is sometimes made to the 'provinces', provincial government was abolished in 1876. Regional government has never been seriously attempted. Central jealousy has combined with local jealousies to destroy it.

Local government was reformed in the 1980s by the Labour government. But, while its reconstruction in general reduced the number of local authorities, it took care to keep the largest city, Auckland (once called the Queen City, now in these degendered days, the City of Sails), divided. Four new cities were created in that metropolis of one million people, in order to make sure that the whole was less than the sum of the parts. The government, moved to Wellington in the nineteenth century, wanted no challenge from the north ('beyond the Bombay hills'). Aucklanders have no local authority with which they might identify or which might have a city-wide responsibility for the facilities they want. New Zealand's whole population is no larger than that of a single big city. But it ensures that its biggest city has no single government of its own.

If efficiency was the alleged aim of the restructuring of local government, the values of the market lay behind other changes. Transport and power, for example, were made over to semi-commercial entities, spurred to compete. In this process, as in the restructuring of local government, the voice of the citizen was often lost. The role of elected representatives, once too large, became too small. Accountability was a watch word: but the new bodies could make commercial sensitivity a ground for secrecy.

The central government is, of course, based on elections, held every three years. But there is very little check on it between elections.

Elections were once a kind of cargo cult. Promises were made. 'We are doing our bust to falfoul the mendit we were govern by the purple', says Fairburn's Right Returnable Mr Selvedge. But that concept is outmoded. Governments now make a virtue of making no promises. If they have made them, they make a virtue of breaking them. It is seen as 'courageous'. It shows that they are determined to govern, giving the New Zealand purple what it kneads not what it wonts.

Not only are there no effective local governments; there has been no second house since the 1950s. A victorious party can rule more or less unchallenged. The party is likely to be dominated by the caucus.

Ministries – cabinet plus non-cabinet members – are large enough to dominate the caucus. Power can thus be exercised by a very few ministers, dominating the cabinet.

Political and constitutional factors are reinforced by economic and social ones. In a small society there are colossi like Dick Seddon. In the depression Michael Joseph Savage acquired the charisma that Fairburn genially sent up. Keith Holyoake managed to know everyone and even make them feel that he cared about everyone. Muldoon played the ordinary Kiwi joker, though no ordinary joker himself. Behind his far from opaque facade was a shrewd intelligence that took every advantage of the media and revelled in the possibilities of personality politics. Yet he, too, perhaps most of all, was like a State Premier: a boss, or, as was said in this dairying country, a milk sheikh. You admired the political skills, but searched in vain for the statesman. 'Think Big' was a description of government projects, but they were not thought through.

It was the Labour government elected in 1984 and re-elected in 1987 that, rather paradoxically, pursued the market-driven reforms that sought to 'restructure' New Zealand's way of doing things, even its way of looking at them. The basic idea was not new. In eighteenth-century Japan, Kaiho Seiryo had concluded that everything, including the realm itself, could be considered a commodity with an exchange value. But he and, two centuries later, Friedman and even Baroness Thatcher, were mere talkers compared with the Kiwi doers. New Zealand became once more a social laboratory, which others could watch with a frisson of delight or horror. What made it possible was the extraordinary power the New Zealand Government had. It was not surprising that a government, apparently dedicated to devolution, to competition, to the market and to the consumer, actually became more powerful rather than less. It might decide to reduce its role in health or welfare. But it decided.

The government had long been known as the fastest lawmaker in the West. Muldoon had piled regulation upon regulation. His successors piled law upon law. The government printer could not keep up (and in the end was sold off). On one occasion amendments were being made to amendments that had not been printed. Friday night – when the parliamentarians would probably want to catch their free flights home – was a favoured time to drive legislation through.

Politicians work very hard, but there is not much sympathy for them. Labour's reforms and Labour's methods produced a triumph for the opposition in 1990. It pursued the same politics. Coca replaced Pepsi. The electorate signified its views by producing an all but hung Parliament in 1993. It also decided to change the system of elections from U.K.-style 'simple majorities' to German-style 'MMP'. The choice had been between more politicking and more reform from above. Despite their sporting instincts, the Kiwis abandoned 'first past the post'. But the change may mean more of the same. There will be more politicians. Will they be more responsive?

Government reforms had stopped short indeed of reforming central government itself. Geoffrey Palmer had written a book he titled '*Unbridled Power?*', but, though publishing a second edition with a title that left out the question mark, he did little to carry out his suggestions when he became Deputy Prime Minister and Prime Minister and some expect a third edition with an exclamation mark. The Treasury, which enjoyed the franchise for Friedmanesque ideology in New Zealand and is even more dominant than the Treasury in the U.K. and Australia, failed to apply its own criteria for others to itself. Quis custodiet indeed.

Pressure groups, of course, exist and Treasury resented 'capture' of the political debate by 'interested parties', even if (or especially if) they might be best informed. But where government is so strong, organisations are relatively weak. The government may subsidise them or include them in its legislation or its members may more or less depend on it. And while the 'old school tie' may not be openly worn, the 'old boy' (and 'old girl') relationships are strong in a small society. Too much is known about everyone. If you sneeze in Auckland, someone will send you a Snowtex (Kleenex) from Dunedin. X went to school with Y: and he was no good at school either. Z was an All Black and his wife is the daughter of the Chief Executive.

The media see themselves in many Western countries as a defence of democracy, although those in Britain seem to content themselves with attacking monarchy. New Zealand's press is middle-of-the road, like most of its drivers. There is no national newspaper, although the Auckland one is titled as if it made the claim. All are based in the main cities: few face the competition that they generally echo government in lauding. TV handles news like a game, biffing disasters to and fro between two announcers. Only National radio provides for any real debate, although politicians sometimes risk (and perhaps enjoy) radio talkbacks (or putdowns).

Who rules New Zealand? The reforms have reduced its independence on the outer world, never great, however, and, prior to them, already diminishing. Inside the country, look to the 'Beehive', the Terrace, Lambton Quay, central Wellington. Break into the cocktail circuit, go to an opening. Then you can find out whether the report has reached the minister's desk and what redundancy the Chief Executive Officer is to be paid: 'Who loses and who wins; who's in, who's out', 'the mystery of things', as Lear puts it. If you want to know.

In a classic manoeuvre, Labour coupled international reform with external excitement. New Zealand had no shortage of energy and it could do without nuclear generation. Now it declared itself nuclear-free, even to the extent of excluding from its ports the nuclear-powered battleships of its allies. American opposition only made the government more assertive. The French blew up a Greenpeace vessel, the *Rainbow Warrior*, in Auckland harbour. But the mouse could not do much more than roar. That it did again when the French announced the renewal of nuclear testing in the Pacific in 1995.

Francophobia

Weak abroad, strong at home, the New Zealand Government could be helped abroad and restrained at home by some of its lawyers. Its international lawyers were distinguished. In New Zealand, the highest courts provided some protection against high-handed government. Appeals still lie with the Privy Council in London. But that court is under sentence of death, so far as New Zealand is concerned.

Of Markets, Managers and Massage Parlours

The governments since 1984 have sought to make the market rule, although they still want to be the unseen body that moves the unseen hand (and rule). They believed that deregulation would bring efficiency and indeed prosperity. They even believed that the leaders of New Zealand commerce would bring efficiency to other activities, which could be turned into business and efficient ones. It was something you had to have faith in, because there was certainly no certainty.

'Our local malefacturers must be incorriged and we must do our boast to increase the voluble prediction of goods.' Thus Fairburn's Mr Selvedge.

Sheltered by tariffs and quotas deriving from the days of import substitution, manufacturers had little urge to upgrade or even maintain standards. It would be a little unfair to use Dr Johnson's phrase about women preaching and dogs standing on their hind legs: it is not done well but you are surprised to find it done at all. Some things were done well ('Well Made New Zealand' was the manufacturers' slogan) and it would be unjust to be surprised about that. But, if manufacturers, given so small a market, could at times produce goods of quality, efficiency was not a word to characterise industry or commerce. Delivery dates were guesses. She'll be right. Private enterprise was often more aptly described as 'the private sector'. And it was not very private.

Deregulation was supposed to shake the Kiwis out of it. Perhaps it did. Certainly a great deal of New Zealand's protected industry collapsed when it faced international competition and many Kiwis were 'shaken out' of their jobs. Unemployment, hardly known in the 1950s, emerging in the 1970s, unchecked by Muldoon's 'Think Big' projects, became an apparently permanent feature of Kiwi life in the 1990s. The competition, of course, may have been quite unfair. The products came from industries with larger capital and larger markets and, of course, in some cases from Asian countries where the work force was deeply unrewarded, if not virtually enslaved. But these things do not prick the consciences of the late twentieth century as much as they did the consciences of the nineteenth. What goes on in other countries is our business only in the commercial sense. Otherwise, it is theirs. And if the President of the U.S. does indeed try to interfere, in the name of human rights, it is not something that the leaders of a little country like New Zealand can be expected to do much about.

One or two of the major firms in New Zealand did rather well. Others survived. Some crashed in October 1987. Overseas investors picked up bargains in the commercial sector, particularly in urban property. And overseas operators did well from the government's determination to sell the family silver. Some went pretty cheap: governments are good at buying dear and selling cheap. And some were still quasi-monopolies. The practice seemed at times to recall, not the age of Adam Smith (or Kaiho Seiryo) but the age of James I, as the private bidders acquired what were public functions, the national airline, telecommunications, the railways. James I was against smoking, too.

Competition could hardly compete. And it was not clear that the urge to run enterprises in a more businesslike manner, which competition was supposed to promote, would survive. Competitors aim to beat their rivals and preferably eliminate them. Meanwhile the government sought to encourage the approach in other sectors, like health and education, where there were other objectives and a simple-minded faith in the efficiency that competition was supposed to produce was in any case irrelevant.

An air of efficiency was certainly promoted, if not the actuality. Yuppies, cellphones, electronic mail, faxes, e-mail, computers: it was all there. New names were murmured (and shouted), like incantations that invoked change, even if they did not indicate it. The Main Roads Department was transmuted into Transit New Zealand

and the broadcasting authority became New Zealand on Air and the Auckland Power Board Mercury Energy. Designing logos became itself a profitable venture, as the epidemic of logorrhea spread. Consultancy, too, was a profitable line. The new jigsaw had to be fitted together; the new bodies needed expertise. That had to be bought (buying is easier than thinking). And it came at a price. Intermediaries flourished and took care to ensure that their reports advocated further investigation, probably more elaborate and certainly more expensive.

The proud Kiwi hardly knew whether to be proud of this transformation or not. It was the wonder of the world, for sure. The world might, however, do no more than wonder. Were the Kiwis showing their sophistication or their naïveté?

One answer was to export their expertise. If they succeeded, the Kiwis would indeed have created the level playing field the economists spoke of (though what game they had in mind was never clear: surely not cricket). But – though hailed in the *Australian Financial Review* as 'the most exciting politician either Australia or New Zealand has produced in the past 20 years' – Sir Roger Douglas was unlikely to convert those who did not believe in GATT and had no intention of dropping their barriers or confessing their subsidies. His new party is called ACT. Will it put up a convincing performance?

Nor perhaps are there more believers in a flat earth than there are in a flat tax. New Zealand did not itself manage to introduce the single level of income tax Douglas wanted, but did introduce two rather low rates.

It had, however, also introduced GST and, unlike VAT and other systems, it applied to all goods and every transaction. Books and magazines are not exempt, nor is food or fuel. And if you pay a fine, that is treated as a service and taxable, too. The result is that the government collects as much in tax as before, if not more, but collects rather more of it from the relatively poor and rather less from the relatively rich.

Is it all a success story? Prime Minister Lange, as Denis Welch put it in 1986, had a vision of the welfare state, not as a sort of dairy godmother, but as a 'liberating element in our lives'. Superannuitants would be relieved of cash, public servants of jobs, the Labour Party 'freed from all that it ever stood for'. Capitalists must be allowed to make money. Ever since, Kiwis have looked for the slowing up of the slowing down and an upturn in the downturn. Has the recession (in indecent phrase) 'bottomed out'? 'Now', says the *Australian Financial Review,* 'new bistros are proliferating, as they were before the 1987 crash.' We are all capitalists now, Sir William Harcourt might say.

Napoleon, with a Bonapartisan sniff, dismissed the British as a nation of shopkeepers. He might have said the same of the Kiwis. There still are plenty of shops, but their nature has changed. The small grocer has been largely displaced by the supermarket (though the hypermarket is still to come). He or she holds on in the form of specialty food shops and in the form of 'dairies' (sometimes rather paradoxically called 'superettes'), now run mostly by Fijian Indian exiles (the equivalent of Britain's patelleries). The former offer local or imported

delicacies, the latter a bit of everything edible, including milk, at almost any time of the day. But you pay for rarity in the one case and convenience in the other.

Competition has introduced another feature which competition is not supposed to produce. Shopkeepers specialise less. Thus you can buy a variety of groceries in a petrol station and you can buy stamps (but not petrol) in the dairy. You can buy wine in the supermarket (but not on Sundays). You can even get Christmas crackers in the Post Office. But no longer does it serve as the people's bank nor as a contact with their government.

It was different 10 years or so ago. Shopping hours were shorter. One late night (until 8.00 or 9.00) was common, but, dairies apart, shops were generally shut on Saturdays and certainly on Sundays. The weekend was a long one, even apart from the long weekends (the Kiwis still take two days off if Christmas and Boxing Day fall on Saturday and Sunday).

Is it indeed like the Weimar Germany of the 1920s where everything was for sale? You can get massage, but a massage parlour is, or at least may be, a brothel. Saunas and gyms may also provide a range of services other than those their name explicitly indicates. But the Kiwis are not alone in euphemisms like escort services or in blatancies like striptease. GST is no doubt charged, in any case.

Credit cards are discreet. They are in wide use. But for them the inflation of the 1970s and 1980s would have been impossible. As it is the cent has no coin. The smallest coin is five cents. It is the age of plastic.

Of Education and Training

Mervyn Cull was sceptical about the Labour government's public opinion poll on education. 'Hopefully, in the medium term it will produce a one-off bottom-line package in terms of ongoing learning experience in the caring, supportive class-room situation ...'

Education everywhere has to survive the educationists and their jargon. The best that can be said of them is that it is difficult to learn about learning. It may not be the worst that can be said of them that they are the prey of fashion and careerism.

New Zealand is subject to the fashions that come from overseas in this field as in others. It has, one is tempted to say all the same, established a serviceable and even in parts, a distinguished education system.

Not a pressure-cooker system, like the British, nor an extravagant one, like the American.

Education in New Zealand has not escaped the attention of government, any more than it has in other Western countries. Unwilling to blame themselves for faltering economies and politically unable to blame employers (or unemployers, as some of them might be better described), governments can blame teachers.

Friedperson theorising and the jargon of the economists were added to those of the educationists to provide an ideology for the 1980s. Education and training were the same thing. They had to serve the market and not be distracted by the prejudices, or even the professionalism, of the 'providers'. The interests of the 'consumer' should prevail, though it might be difficult to determine who the consumer was and better therefore to talk of 'stakeholders'.

Treasury and the reformers of the 1980s used this newspeak avidly and it had the usual effect of bad currency. Education was not, like margarine, manufactured and consumed and nothing was gained by claiming that it was. Except, for some, power. A revolution leads to a redistribution of power. In New Zealand, that tends to mean a new set of bureaucrats, now there to monitor rather than inspect, to hold teachers accountable rather than responsible, to articulate objectives, measure outputs and establish quality assurance mechanisms.

Yet while the market ruled and the language of the market was chattered, education clearly was a realm it found difficult to penetrate, as the elaboration of the government's continued intervention tended to show.

Marketeers continued to lament. Clearer 'signals' would enable students (or parents) to act rationally and choose to invest in the education that would bring them success and satisfaction. But what signals could the market give about employment five or 10 years later? And how did the rational 15-year-old (or parent) balance personal satisfaction and future earning?

No doubt New Zealand had to 'compete' and it is a reasonable supposition, though there is no proof, that a better educated work force sharpens a nation's 'cutting edge' in the 'global market'. But, while they had by no means abandoned intervention, New Zealand governments were unwilling to plan for the future, or even to prognosticate in the way successful competitors had done in East Asia, the economic success of which was so much admired. Extending the leaving age – from a surprisingly low 15 to a still modest 16 and now up to 17 – might help at least to keep the kids (the Kiwi word for school pupils) off the streets. Indeed, the increasing numbers staying on in the higher forms and going into tertiary education were in part the result of unemployment. But they were welcomed by teachers at both levels. The universities (varsity in New Zealand, uni in Australia), which had long sustained the concept of 'open entry', greatly expanded their rolls in the 1980s and 1990s. some are now very large: the University of Auckland has 25,000 students.

Paying for it all was another matter. Industrialists, as in Britain, were famously unwilling: these were men (mostly) who did not want to pay the piper, but did want to call the tune. Government wanted to curb

expenditure: more scholar per dollar, as Colin Mackerras would put it. Ideology suggested the individual should pay. Recognising that that made no political sense at the school level, the theorists had to try to make sense of it at the tertiary level. One step was to run the institutions even more leanly. Another was to charge higher fees after the economists had loyally decided that the 'benefits' of tertiary education, unlike those of secondary, were 'private' rather than 'public' goods. The third was student loans. In these the commercial sector, risk-averse, displayed no interest. The government stepped in, managing to persuade itself that the loans could be stated as assets for the benefit of the auditors (though they were also stated as grants for the benefit of the electorate).

The reforms were also designed to encourage more private initiatives in education. Education in New Zealand has been overwhelmingly a state function and it still is. There are some private schools (New Zealand does not follow Britain in calling its private schools public schools) and there are some Catholic schools in a half-way or more than half-way house ('integrated'). A few of the secondary schools – generally those in the wealthier parts of the main cities – see themselves as élite schools and to some extent are schools for the élite, often, like the private schools, borrowing features from the English public schools (at least as described in novels and memoirs).

Loyalty to the school indeed counts in New Zealand. People seem to recall their period at school, secondary, or even primary, with a nostalgia that is expressed in centenary celebrations and reunions. The place is small enough for New Zealanders to recall that the Prime Minister was in the form above them at secondary school. Was he a prefect? More important, did he play for the First XV?

There is far less nostalgia about the universities. Their growth is, of course, relatively recent and most of New Zealand's leaders have not been graduates. A change in one trend may not bring a change in the other. The Labour government of the 1980s contained more graduates than any previous cabinet. But such familiarity as they had acquired with the universities bred what familiarity is usually said to breed.

Their 'reforms' of the universities did, however, elicit protest from other graduates. Some of it arose from real sympathy with the institutions and their attempts to sustain academic freedom and carry out research. Some, perhaps, also came from sheer distrust of political and bureaucratic controls, which were seen to be expanding even (or especially) when the ostensible aim was to roll back the state.

New Zealand has its own version of 'back to basics': reeling and writhing and arithmetic, as the Mock Turtle put it, ambition, distraction, uglification and derision. Rather surprisingly for a country that is so concerned with the past, it has downplayed History: it is not taught at school before Form 5 and is nowhere compulsory.

Education was once designed to integrate the Maori by assimilation. Now it tries to take a bicultural approach. Maori themselves took the initiative to set

up schools that teach only in Maori (kohanga reo, kura kaupapa). Whether that will increase the numbers of Maori in tertiary education remains to be seen. At present they number less than half of what demography suggests they might.

Envoi

> New Zealanders have the minds of children and the passions of men .... Futurity is seldom looked into .... Fondness of novelty is a passion, but it is almost impossible to excite wonder. In imitation they are strong and from mimicry derive pleasure .... When mastered, either physically or mentally, they become manageable as children.

Those remarks were made by a European historian about the Maori in 1855. In some respects they are not unlike some of the comments offered about New Zealanders more generally in the foregoing pages. It is indeed difficult to write of peoples without patronage.

Not that nineteenth-century colonists were in general trying very hard. The British Government had intervened in New Zealand and, on behalf of Queen Victoria, made a Treaty at Waitangi in 1840. In the eyes of settlers, that did not provide adequately for their wish for land, land and more land: the Queen's government, they felt, 'only appeared on the scene as the friend and protector of aborigines' (Reeves). Eventually war was to arbitrate in their favour, although, as James Belich has pointed out, the Maori put up a good fight.

At the end of the century, the settlers often spoke of the Maori as a dying race. In fact, that may have been wishful thinking: it was certainly not true after the 1890s, though the obelisk on Auckland's One Tree Hill, a 'memorial to the Maori race', dates from 1939.

At the same time, the settlers congratulated themselves on the harmony between the races in New Zealand. Indeed Maori and European leaders jointly opposed the entry of the yellow race. The Maori were in a sense honorary whites, certainly superior to other coloured races. That race relations were better than in other colonies may have been true. But the competition was not strong.

Seeking a Kiwi identity, Europeans were sometimes tempted to find it in Maoridom. Maori haka were used, or misused, by rugby teams (often, indeed, substantially Maori). There was a risk that the rituals of Maori society would become not merely a display for visiting dukes, but a titillation for tourists. The syllabus in Maori schools was assimilated to that in the state schools. Maori was not taught, but relegated to a rural folk language, as Bruce Biggs, a Maori Professor of Maori, put it.

After the world wars – in which Maori played a distinguished role – the relationship changed. New Maori leaders emerged and especially from the 1950s more Maori migrated to the towns.

The reforms of the 1980s changed the position of the Maori, as of everyone else. In particular the role of the Waitangi Tribunal was expanded, with the task of redeeming the pledges of the Treaty. Assimilation was replaced by biculturalism. Some called the country New Zealand/Aotearoa as a symbol of this hyphenation.

The government of the 1970s was devoted to 'Think Big' projects: vast investments seemed to be the answer. The government of the 1990s still thinks big, although along different lines. It wants 'solutions': a single qualifications framework; a final settlement of the Waitangi claims, unromantically termed the 'fiscal envelope'. Maori wanted to see the back of that envelope.

There was cynicism, there was idealism; as there long had been, there were dealers and double dealers. But Maori and Pakeha already shared many views, many values, many of the quirks and quiddities described in this book.

That offered some reason to hope that New Zealand might after all lead the world. If 3.5m people cannot make a go of it, who can?

About the Author

Born in England at the height (or depth) of the Depression, Nicholas Tarling went to Australia in 1957. No one goes so far as he knows not where he is going, as Oliver Cromwell put it.

Since 1965 he has lived in New Zealand. He is thus a (bloody) Pom, a Commonwealth citizen, a rootless cosmopolitan, and some kind of Kiwi. Certainly some of his best friends are Kiwis. Or were.

Professor of History and Public Orator at The University of Auckland, and for a long period Dean of Arts, he likes teaching and he hates marking. He is a keen defender of traditional university values, and, in 1994 with Ruth Butterworth, published *A Shakeup*

Anyway, Government and the Universities in New Zealand in a Decade of Reform.

Unmarried and insomniac, he has also published a dozen books on Southeast Asian history, broadcast on opera, and practised the fine art of coarsely acting in over a hundred plays.

Faced with compulsory retirement, he is developing an interest in recycling. His only other exercise is an antiquated but all-weather breast-stroke.